W: The First 100 Days

A White House Journal

W:

The First 100 Days

A White House Journal

by

D. B. Gilles

&

Sheldon Woodbury

Andrews McMeel Publishing

Kansas City

W: The First 100 Days

01 02 03 04 05 BAM 10 9 8 7 6 5 4 3 2 1

ISBN: 0-7407-1836-3

Library of Congress Card Number: 2001-086445

Book design by Holly Camerlinck

For William Jefferson Clinton
and Albert Gore Jr.

—*D. B. Gilles*

For LuAnn Woodbury, the love of my life,
and my parents. And a special thanks to
D. B. Gilles, a great friend.
Also, to everyone in the Department of
Dramatic Writing at New York University.

—*Sheldon Woodbury*

Special Acknowledgment
Jane Dystel, our literary agent

I, George W. Bush, hereby declare that this
journal will be an accurate rendering of
my first 100 days as the 44th, I mean, 43rd
President of the United States of America.
In these pages, to the best of my ability,
I will reveal the truth about what transpired
within the hallowed halls of the most powerful
house in the world, because this journal will
be a day-to-day recording of my innermost
thoughts and feelings.

This is my pledge as your President.

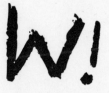

Saturday, January 20, 2001

Got inaugurated today. Cheney was lookin' at me funny when I took the oath. I felt weird bein' younger than him. I wonder if now that I'm President I can ask him why his upper lip tilts to the side?

Sent thank-you notes to the Supreme Court. Everybody thinks my favorite Supremes are Scalia & Rehnquist, but it's really Diana Ross. She rules! Wish I woulda kissed her instead of Oprah.

W ♥ loves O.W.

Gotta come up with my first Presidential act. Maybe get Poppy on Mount Rushmore for his birthday. If Lincoln has to go to make room, then tough toenails. What'd he do anyway, 'cept invent a really neat car?

Called Al Gore. Asked him to introduce me
to Tommy Lee Jones. Ain't no reason
Tommy Lee & I can't be buds. We're both
from Texas. We both went to Harvard. He
was quarterback. I was a cheerleader.

Note To Self: Bein' a guy cheerleader sounds a
little homo. Send a hit man, I mean, a Secret
Service agent to New Haven & get rid of all
photographs of me jumpin' in the air like a
girl or holdin' a pom-pom.

Thing To Remember: Stop calling
Katherine Harris Lily Munster.

Because of the Inauguration festivities Cheney said it was OK to sleep in this mornin', so I did. He also said I could skip the lunch with Nelson Mandela. I thought he died 20 years ago. Wait. That was Nelson Rockefeller.

I wonder if Ozzie Nelson's still alive.

Saw the red button I gotta press if there's a nucular war. Wonder why it's red. Every so often I stare at it. Looks like one a them dots Indian women have on their foreheads.

＊Thing TO Do: Ask Trent Lott if he's related to that guy in the Bible whose wife turned into a pillar of salt.

First big National Security briefing today at 11:30. Hope it's over before The Young & the Restless. It's on the Middle East. I had Laura write all the countries down on my palm. And they said I didn't learn anything at Yale. Go Bulldogs!

Called Jeb & busted his chops that I'm President & he's not. He kept talkin' about the family dynasty. I said I never liked Dynasty. I always preferred Dallas.

Met with my Drug Czar today. He said it was a very serious problem that needs a strong policy. Finally, this is an area I know somethin' about. We agreed that drugs can kill. But I had to remind him that they can also give you nifty ideas like wantin' to become President. Note To Self: Why do they call him Czar? Isn't that a Commie word?

Laura's right. If this whole literacy thing is gonna fly then I should start readin' some books. But she always wants me to practice doin' it without movin' my lips. That's what I get for marryin' a librarian. Hey! That rhymes.

Note To Self: Scrap the new literacy program. Further Note To Self: Could there be a Cliff's Notes program?

Hope Cheney doesn't become a laughin' stock like Poppy's Vice President. Never could understand all the crap Dan Quayle had to take. I thought he was smart as a whip. And deep. And it was so kewl that he looked like Robert Redford. Too bad we had to keep him outa sight durin' the convention and entire campaign. Note To Self: Give Dan a call.

Cheney shot down my idea for a
Presidential act. I still don't see what's
wrong with pardoning Robert Downey Jr.
I know what the boy's goin' through.

Met this really neat foreign leader today.
Forgot his name. He was wearin' a toga like
when I was a frat boy. Nice guy. Gave
me an elephant tusk. Thing To Do: Find out
if Africa's a country or a state. Ask
Clarence Thomas. I think that's where he's from.

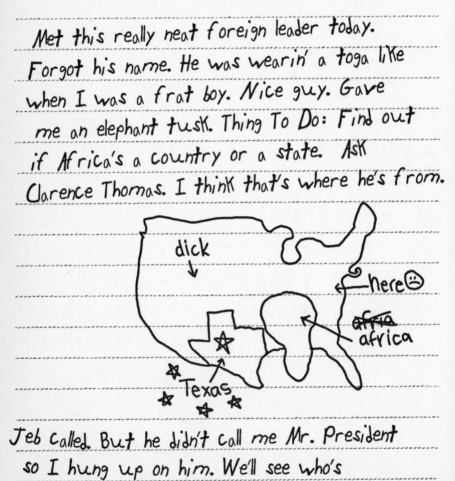

dick

here☹

~~affia~~
africa

Texas

Jeb called. But he didn't call me Mr. President
so I hung up on him. We'll see who's
the smart one.

Had to change my AOL screen name now that I'm President. I don't understand why. When I was Governor it was *NotDubya* & nobody knew it was me in them chat rooms. Now I'm *NotPrez.*

www.W.com

Been thinkin' about Michael Jackson, I mean Jesse Jackson. Don't like him. Nope. Don't like him one bit. Not cuz he's black. I like black people. 'Specially if you got a man on second & you're down two runs in the bottom of the eighth. GO RANGERS!

Time to mend fences with John McCain. Maybe we can share hardship stories. What was tougher? His 5 years in a Vietnamese prison or my 7 weeks in rehab?

The White House chef keeps puttin' beans in the chili. Not only does it ruin the taste but it gives me gas. I let one loose in the Oval Office. Karl Rove was there. We both pretended it was one a them Secret Service guys. Wonder if other Presidents farted in the Oval Office. Bet LBJ cleared the room.

✳ Note To Self: If I write a book, put in a chapter on Presidential windbreaking.

Poppy's startin' to bug me. Hey, I'm the President & he's the former President who's not the President no more. If he keeps this up then no Mount Rushmore. But he did have one good idea today. Get Mother her own postage stamp. That way the whole country'll be kissin' her butt just like we do.

yada yada yada yada yada yada yada yada YADA
yada YADA YADA yada yada yada Yada
YADA yada yada yada yada YADA yada yada yada
yada yada YADA yada yada yada yada yada yadayada
yada yada yada yada yada yada yada yada
yada yada yada yada yada YADA yada yada YADA
YADA yada yada yada yada YADA yada yada yada
yada yada YADA yada yada yada yada yada yada
YADA yada yada yada yada YADA yada yada yada
yada YADA YADA yada yada yada Yada yadayada
yada yada yada yada yada yada yada yada YADA
Yada yada YADA yada yada yada yada yada yada
YADA yada yada yada yada YADA yada yada yada
YADA YADA YADA YADA YADA YADA YADA YADA YADA
yada yada yada yada yada YADA yada yada yada
yada yada yada yada yada yada yada yada YADA yada
Yada yada YADA yada yada yada yada yada
YADA yada yada yada yada YADA yada yada yada
yada yada yada yada yada yada yada yada
yada yada yada yada yada yada yada yada yada
YADA YADA YADA YADA YADA YADA YADA YADA YADA
Yada yada YADA yada yada yada yada yada yada
Yada yada yada yada YADA yada yada yada yadayada
yada yada yada yada yada

Had a weird dream last night. I was givin' a speech to the country & I didn't have no clothes on. But that wasn't the bad part. Sam Donaldson was staring at me & I kinda liked it. If I go homo Poppy'll never forgive me.

Ask Condoleezza what the hell kinda name Condoleezza is.

Had the horseshoe pit put back in the Rose Garden just like Poppy had it when he was King, I mean President. Cheney & I played a game. He conked me in the head. Twice. I always suspected he was an uncoordinated goober. Damn, that upper lip of his frosts my ass.

Laura's got me boning up on my readin' skills. She got me a new Hooked on Phonics. But I still like it better when she reads to me. Tried to read that Harry Potter book. Boy, it was long and heavy.

Time to reward Lily Munster, I mean, Katherine Harris for helping me steal Florida. For starters, I'm thinkin' about a complete makeover at Georgette Klinger.

Note To Self: Find out if a President has to be dead before he gets his face on money. Poppy sure would look Kewl on a thousand dollar bill.

Everybody was worried that the stress of bein' President would make me start drinkin' or snortin' blow again. There is no stress. This is a breeze. If you want to know what stress is try gettin' your brother to get out the vote in the state he's Godfather of, I mean, Governor of.

Dan Quayle returned my phone call today. We exchanged e-mail addresses. Put him on my Buddies List. Dan said I'm the only member of the Republican Party who called him in 4 years. He spends mosta his time these days golfin', like O.J.

Note To Self: Wonder if he ever thought about helpin' O.J. find the real killer or killers.

Thursday, February 1, 2001

Laura got mad when she found out I had one a my Secret Service guys read Harry Potter for me. Kicked me outa bed, so I used the opportunity to spend the night in the Lincoln bedroom. Big deal! The bed's lumpy & Lincoln's picture gave me nightmares. Couldn't get that mole outa my head.

Can't decide if it would be in bad taste to tell Patti Reagan that I had a hardcore crush on her when her Poppy was President & mine was VP. Never cared for Maureen Reagan cuz of her big ass.

Gore won't give me Tommy Lee Jones' home phone number. Thing To Do: Have a CIA agent break into his house & steal it. Also get Jon Bon Jovi's number.

Friday, February 2, 2001

Groundhog Day today. I wanted to introduce a bill makin' it legal to hunt the ugly little bastards & to change the day to Armadillo Day, but Cheney talked me outa it. Cheney talks me outa lotsa things. Cheney talks me into lotsa things too. Sometimes I think Cheney wishes he had my job & I had his. When I think thoughts like that I feel sad.

Sure wish Kathie Lee would come back to Regis and Kathie Lee. I been secretly in love with her since she sang them songs on Name That Tune. Hard to believe she was Jewish. Good thing she got Born Again. It's a nice feelin' Knowin' she's goin' to Heaven.

Bumped into "Senator" Hillary today. Bitch scares the bejesus outa me.

Been waitin' for the right time to challenge Colin Powell to a game of Dungeons & Dragons.

Had dinner with the Queen of England's son Tony Blair. Never met a Prince before. We served him that fish & chips crap which is really fish & french fries. Damn Limeys. The way they butcher the English language.

I like to say Donald Rumsfeld's last name over and over. Rumsfeld. Rumsfeld. Rum...sfeld. Rum...sfeld. Rum. Rum. Rum. Damn, I could go for a pitcher of piña coladas.

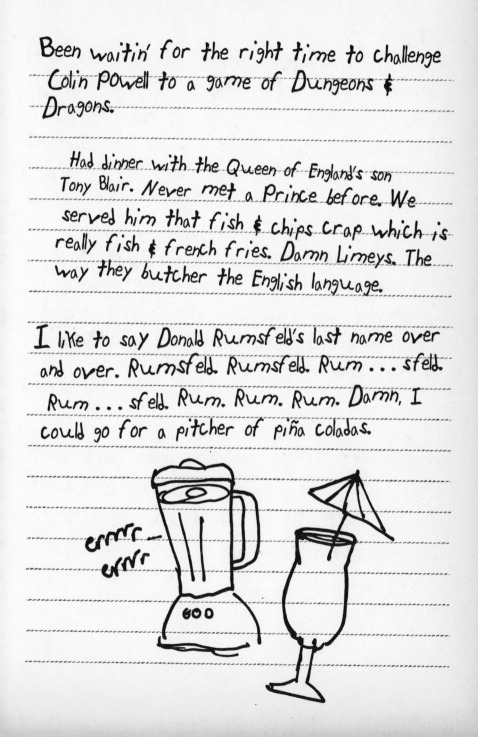

Sunday, February 4, 2001

Thing To Do:
Call Oliver North, I mean, Oliver Stone. I mean, Oliver Hardy. Damn! Whichever one a them Olivers is the guy who made them movies about JFK & Nixon. Ask him to make a movie about Poppy.

Took a walk through the White House. Good to be back. Saw Clinton's portrait next to Poppy's. Satan almost got the better of me cuz I was one step away from grabbin' my Sharpie & drawin' a mustache on Fatboy.

Saw a portrait of Teddy Roosevelt, then a portrait of Franklin Delano Roosevelt. I thought it was just me & Poppy & John Adams & John Quincy Adams that were the only father & son Presidents.

Spring Training started today. I'd be Commissioner of Baseball if Mother didn't want revenge for losin' the '92 election & if Poppy didn't have this thing about us bein' the first family to have 3 Presidents.

Secret Thought: Like Jeb's ever gonna get elected to anything again after that Florida bullshit 'ceptin' maybe dogcatcher.

Guess the Stones were right: "You can't always get want you want, but if you try somehow you get what your parents need."

Tuesday, February 6, 2001

Everybody's so busy around here 'cept me. Ain't got nobody to talk to. I need someone to confide in, so I got me an e-mail buddy to bounce off my thoughts & whatnot. I ain't tellin' nobody who it is cuz I don't want to be chewed out. But his initials are D.Q.

Started workin' on my Enemies List. So far there's Satan, Jim Beam & everybody who didn't vote for me. And Jeb's really startin' to piss me off.

Thing To Find Out:
What does GOP stand for?

Note To Self: Think I been workin' too hard. I never worked this hard in Texas. Need to start schedulin' more free time for myself. Good thing I'm not gettin' paid by the hour. Or am I?

Wonder why they call it the Oval Office. Looks more like a squashed circle.

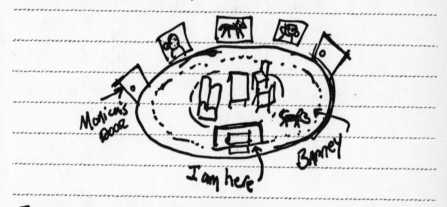

Monica's Booze

I am here

Barney

I keep forgettin' my secret code name. Since I'm a big movie fan, I told the Secret Service to come up with a film that'd be my code name. Figured I wouldn't forget it. They suggested "Clueless," "Barfly" & "Dead Man Walking." I didn't like any of 'em, so I picked my own: "The Empire Strikes Back."

The great thing about bein' in the White House is all the history that's here. Last night one a them Secret Service guys showed me the basement room where Nixon worshipped Satan, Nancy Reagan hid her astrologer & Carter made his brother Billy sleep.

Our new dog Barney was a bribe, I mean, gift from Christine Todd Whitman. He's cute, but he's crappin' everywhere. And he's always tryin' to hump our old dog, Spot. She's nice, but I can't figure out if I'm supposed to call her "Christine," "Todd" or "Whitman."

Cheney's always so serious. Every once in awhile I feel like goosin' him or havin' a food fight or playin' a good game of Twister.

＊*Note To Self:* How many sick days are Presidents allowed each year?

Cheney's always starin' at me. When I catch him he looks away all quicklike. Then I catch him starin' again. It's like he's sizin' me up. I don't mean in no homo way. It's like I'm Bambi & he's a hunter with an AK-47 & he's got me in his sights, but he can't pull the trigger even though he wants to cuz I'm some kinda endangered species.

Thing To Do: If this keeps up I'm goin' over his head & tellin' Karl Rove. If that don't work I'm tellin' Poppy. And if that don't work I'm tellin' Mother.

today. Got real
s. I'll just

Saturday, February 10, 2001

Note To Historians: When I get nervous I like to chew on paper. For some reason it relaxes me. Just like a cold six pack of Lone Star. 'Cept I don't get a buzz with paper unless I eat a lot of it with some ground up *No-Doz* & spin around really fast for a coupla minutes.

Chen
I fee
playin' a

Sunday, February 11, 2001

A leader's gotta stay in shape. That's why I try to jog every day. And I look a helluva lot better in joggin' shorts than my unemployed predecessor did. He ran like a sissy. I run like a man. He ran like a 12-year-old girl in a training bra. I run like a noble gladiator gallopin' through the streets of Washington D.C. And I don't wear no jockstrap either.

Take that, Slick!

Since I'm a uniter & not a divider, maybe I should try to get the Beatles back together. Or the Monkees. Or The Partridge Family. Danny Bonaduce was so kewl!

Was gonna alphabetize my Rolodex today. Got real bored after about 20 minutes. I'll just call Information.

Monday, February 12, 2001

Findin' difficult solutions to difficult problems: That's what a leader does. Take last night for instance. Willie Nelson was here. After a fine rib dinner Willie wanted to smoke some weed. Not a good idea, I said. This is the White House. I could get in trouble if Laura found out. So we went up on the roof. Bitchin' view.

Today's Lincoln's birthday. Once you've slept in his bedroom the star quality ain't the same. OK, I guess that Emanualholyfield Proclamation looks good on a resume, but after that, I mean, what'd he do? OK, there's the Continental & and the Town Car & that tunnel in New York... It'd be soooo Kewl if they'd name a tunnel after me.

Creepy Thought: Does Gary Bauer look like an alien or what?

Even Creepier Thought: What if Gary Bauer IS a freakin' alien?

Thing To Do Fast In The Interest Of National Security: Tell Condoleezza to find out if Bauer was anywhere near Roswell, New Mexico, when that UFO crashed in 1947.

Thing To Find Out: What does an elephant have to do with the Republican Party? And what's with the Democrats & that donkey?

Valentine's Day. Maybe I should go on national TV & tell everybody I love 'em. But I don't. Screw it.

D.Q. e-mailed me an electronic Valentine's Day card. Wasn't no homo thing, just a simple greeting:

> To the Leader of the Free
> World from a guy who was
> a <u>heartbeat</u> away from bein'
> Leader of the Free World.

Thing To Do: Better stop bustin' Ashcroft's 'nads for gettin' beat by a dead guy. That is soooo harsh, but soooo kewl.

Thursday, February 15, 2001

This is my horse. He's my best friend in
the whole world. Around him I don't hafta pretend
I'm not dyslexic & that I have ADD.
He don't care if I use the wrong words or say
things that don't make sense. He just loves
me for who I am. A regular guy who likes to
hunt, fish, play video games & keep to myself.
Sometimes I wish he & I could just
ride outa this town & head on home
to Crawford.

It's Kewl havin' my own airplane. Made some small modifications. Not sure why they call it Air Force One.

John McCain can Kiss my Presidential ass. Campaign finance reform ain't gonna happen. It bites major donkey dong. How the hell does he think I became President in the first place? Hey John-Mr.-5-Years-In-A-POW-Camp-War-Hero-With-A-Nasty-Temper. Can you spell REPUBLIKANN FATT CAATS?

Thing To Do: Call Steven Spielberg & ask him if he's interested in making Jaws 4. It'd be about a Great White Shark that terrorized Washington D.C. & eats Maureen Dowd.

Saturday, February 17, 2001

✱ Super Important Thing To Do: Presidents' Day is on the 19th. Find out if I get the day off. ✱

Condoleezza's a brilliant woman, but every time I see her I can't help thinkin' she should be singin' backup for Tina Turner.

Thing To Do: Make list of actors who will play Poppy, me & Jeb in the movie about us. First choices are:
   Poppy: Kirk Douglas
   Me: Michael Douglas
   Jeb: Tom Arnold

Thing To Do: Find out who I gotta call to get tomorrow off.

Made a Presidential decision about the toilet paper in the Oval Office crapper. They got Scott tissue in there instead of Charmin. I like the Charmin cuz it feels nice & it's fun to squeeze. Almost as much fun as them plastic bubble things that come in packages.

Gotta come up with a title for Poppy's movie. So far, only thing that comes to me is Bush. Who'd go to see a movie called Bush 'ceptin' maybe some gardeners?

Today's Presidents' Day. All the poor workin' stiffs get the day off but I don't. They get to take advantage of them neat sales at all the stores.

Thing To Do: Find out the exact hours a President's supposed to work. Nobody ever told me when to come in, when to leave, when I can take my breaks, when I should go to lunch, if I'm allowed to make personal phone calls. There should be a manual on this. Maybe I should write a manual on this stuff.

Did some soul-searchin' last night. Started thinkin' 'bout my legacy. What do I want to be remembered for? Had some good ideas, but I didn't write 'em down. Only one I recall is that it'd be kewl to be remembered as the guy responsible for gettin' the Rock & Roll Hall of Fame outa Cleveland.

Tuesday, February 20, 2001

Been President for a month now. They say the first 100 days is s'posed to be a honeymoon for me. Horsepucky. Don't feel like I'm on a honeymoon. Feels more like I'm in one a them Outward Bound Tough Love Camps for teenagers with drug problems.

Met with the National Rifle Association guys today. Charlton Heston is so Kewl. He said I could call him Chuck. I asked him who he liked playin' better, Ben-Hur, the astronaut in Planet of the Apes or Spartacus. He said he wasn't in Spartacus. I felt like a boob.

Note To Self: Ask Chuck if he'd be interested in playin' Poppy in the movie. And ask him if he can pull some Hollywood strings & get Jack Nicholson to play me. Jack's even Kewler than Chuck. As for playin' Jeb, Tom Arnold, definitely. Or maybe Gary Coleman.

Find out if I get my birthday off.
Gonna be 55. Wonder if there's an age
limit on bein' Baseball Commissioner.

Saw Cheney put somethin' in my Dr. Pepper
during our Quiet Time afternoon nap. Next
thing I knew he was sittin' in _my_ chair at
_my_ desk talkin' on _my_ Hot Line starin' at my
red nucular war button talkin' to Poppy tellin'
him "Things are working out just as planned,
sir." I pretended to be asleep. Sometimes I
wonder if Cheney likes Poppy more than me.

Saw this movie called <u>Dave</u> about a regular
guy who looks like the President & is hired to
impersonate him after he has a stroke.
Wish I could find somebody to impersonate
me, 'specially at press conferences.

Thursday, February 22, 2001

Today's George Washington's birthday. Wonder if I'll ever be as great as him. We have one thing in common besides our first names. Wonder if my stonewallin' about whether I used drugs'll be as famous a story as him BSin' about choppin' down that friggin' lemon tree.

D.Q. & I are becomin' fast friends. We IM each other 15 or 16 times a day. Too bad he & Poppy got beat in '92. He coulda been President in '96 & now he'd be into his second term & I'd be Baseball Commissioner & there'd be no "Senator" Hillary & no Barney leavin' turds everywhere.

J. C Watts finally told me what his initials stand for. Julius Caesar. I didn't Know he was Italian.

Friday, February 23, 2001

Friday, February 23, 2001

Dow Jones industrial average

```
11200
11100
11000
10900
10800
10700
10600
10500
10400
10300
10200
10100
10000
 9900
```

10,578.24
Down 935

```
 7                          23
Jan.                       Feb.
```

Source: The Associated Press

Clinton used to say "It's the economy, stupid" &
now I feel like he's talkin' directly to me. And
this is what happened to Poppy. The economy
tanked & he got the big boot. Gotta stay calm.
Not panic. Think rational thoughts.

I want my puppy!

Here's a little souvenir I got from a recent visitor to the White House—Dolly Parton. I been thinkin'. Heck with Poppy. Let's put them torpedoes on Mount Rushmore!

Cheney says I gotta have some big Presidential act durin' my first 100 days. None a these high-powered guys I appointed have come up with jackshit. And when I get a good idea everybody thinks it's dumb. Like today I said why don't we invade Cuba, capture their best pitchers & bring Elian Gonzalez back.

Find out exactly what Condoleezza's job is as National Security Advisor. Wonder if it means she's gonna install those machines that beep when you walk through with stolen merchandise or that everybody gets frisked.

Sunday, February 25, 2001

Spielberg passed on my <u>Jaws 4</u> idea, but he said if I had any other stories I could take a meetin' with him. That is so Kewl. The most powerful man in the world meetin' with the most powerful man in Hollywood.

Maybe we could form a club.

Already got another idea. Wonder if Steve'll be interested in a sequel to <u>E.T.</u> called <u>W.G.</u> It's about an alien boy who finds himself lost & confused in a terrible place called Notgnihsaw CD. All he wants to do is go back home to his friendly planet Texas, I mean, Saxet, & be Commissioner of Baseball.

W.G. The Texaterrestrial

Here's a little souvenir I got from a recent visitor to The White House—Dolly Parton. I been thinkin'. Heck with Poppy. Let's put them torpedoes on Mount Rushmore!

Cheney says I gotta have some big Presidential act durin' my first 100 days. None a these high-powered guys I appointed have come up jackshit. And when I get a good idea everybo thinks it's dumb. Like today I said why don't invade Cuba, capture their best pitchers Elian Gonzalez back.

Find out exactly what Condoleezz as National Security Advisor. W means she's gonna install those mac when you walk through with st or that everybody gets frisked

Tuesday, February 27, 2001

Note To Historians: As the past day proves, even the friggin' White House can run outa toilet paper.

Note To Self: Find out who's in charge a buyin' the Charmin & have Cheney drill him a new bumhole.

Rum...sfeld...Rum...sfeld...Rum...sfeld

Rum...sfeld Rum...

RUM...RUM.

Oliver Stone called & said Poppy didn't do anything big enough to have a feature film made about him. What the hell's with him? Did he forget about the Golf War & that Poppy killed Saddam Hussein?

Glad that Laura don't have a dumb name like Tipper or Ladybird. Laura's a sensible name like Barbara, Nancy or Betty.

Note To Self: Good thing I didn't marry nobody named Condoleezza.

Thursday, March 1, 2001

Weird how February is shorter than other months. Kinda like how Tom Delay's shorter than other Congressmen.

Gotta case a the blahs today. Don't know what it is. Maybe I should stop watchin' them late-night guys on TV. They make fun a me every night. And it's always about how stupid I am. All's I gotta say is if I'm so stupid, why am I the Principal of the United Freakin' States?

EPA, HUD, HEW. All these initials of the different cabinet posts are drivin' me crazy. Thing To Do: Get some interns to find out what they mean. And while they're at it, have 'em find out what IHOP stands for.

Everybody's excited about who I picked for my Cabinet. They say it looks like America: different ethnic groups & sexes. Duh! This isn't an episode of <u>Friends</u>. This is the Cabinet advisin' the Leader of the Free World. It's just like golf. I swing the club, but I need somebody else to carry my bags.

Karl Rove told me that a deli in Georgetown named a sammich after me. It's two pieces of white bread with nothin' in the middle. That sure don't sound like good eats to me.

Wonder if Alan Greenspan is related to the guy who owns C-SPAN.

Saturday, March 3, 2001

Feeling a little philosophical today. Got the legs up
on the desk thinkin' about the Big Picture.
Lots of complex issues to ponder. Taxes, health
care, foreign policy. Got the door closed. No
appointments for awhile. Maybe it's time to
do some heavy thinkin'... Hey! What happened?
What time is it? Whew! Musta dozed off! This
day just flew by!

Thing To Do: Create a Senate sub-committee to find out once & for all what the lyrics are to "Louie, Louie."

Came up with a few more possible actors for the movie about Poppy.

    Poppy: Paul Newman
    Me: Harrison Ford
    Jeb: Tom Arnold

Got bored so I called one a them Psychic Hotlines. Grace, my psychic adviser, told me to beware of an ex-First Lady with powerful aspirations. Can't decide if she means Hillary or Mother.

Thing To DO:
  Call Colin, J.C, Condoleezza & Clarence & invite
'em to come over & watch the <u>Good Times</u>
  marathon with me on Nickelodeon. That
Jimmy Walker is so Kewl!

"DYNO-MITE!!!"

Note To Self: Re-think the <u>Good Times</u> marathon
party. Might be considered racist. Better get some
  white people there too. Maybe Wayne Newton
& Michael Jackson.

Went swimmin' in the presidential pool last night.
Lots of history in there. That's where Kennedy
used to go skinny dippin' with Marilyn Monroe.
But I don't believe in that Kinda sinful stuff.
It was just me & my dogs, Barney & Spot,
  spendin' some quality time together.

Never too early to start gatherin' stuff for my Presidential library.

Phillips Academy
Andover, Massachusettes

Pupil: _George W. Bush_

Academic Achievement

Reporting Period	1	2	3	4
READING	D	D	F	D
LANGUAGE	F	D	D	F
MATHEMATICS	D	D	D	D
HISTORY	F	F	F	F
GEOGRAPHY	F	F	F	F
SCIENCE	D	D	D	F

Teacher Notes:

George is a very friendly boy, but not the brightest apple in the tree. Luckily, he doesn't let his mental deficiencies get in his way. He's a leader in the class. For instance, he's always the first one to fall asleep during naptime every day and that sets a very good example.

Brought my Twister game to the Joint Chiefs of Staff meetin' today. Figured if things got as boring as the last few sessions we could take a break & have some laughs. Shit. Bastards all stared at me like I was Gomer Pyle.

* Note To Self: Invite Jim Nabors, Don Knotts & Andy Griffith to lunch. And Opie. Shit. Opie's a big-time director now.

Thing To Do: Contact Opie, I mean, Ron Howard, about Poppy's movie.

Thursday, March 8, 2001

Note To Self: Why can I write my name perfectly when nobody's lookin', but I always mess it up when I gotta do it in public? Like today when I had to sign the new Literacy bill.

Note To Historians: Please ignore the Wite-Out on all my public documents.

That damn Gary Bauer was in here today. Nobody believes me, but I know that little shit is a friggin' alien cut loose from some mothership. Look at his eyes. His forehead. Reminds me a that creature in the <u>Alien Autopsy</u> video.

Note To Historians: My advisers are still sweatin' bullets about whether or not I really won Florida. They don't know what we'll do if the recount shows that Gore really won. They're all afraid that "Mr. Fashion Plate, David Boies," will come back locked & loaded. Not to worry, I tell 'em. My friends on the Supreme Court have already ruled that this election's way too important to be decided just by the way people voted.

Saturday, March 10, 2001

Gettin' the blahs again. Nobody talks to me
& Cheney ordered my Secret Service guys
not to play with me. I feel like it's
Thanksgiving Day & I ain't allowed to eat
with the grown-ups.

Damn Barney peed on my journal.
Startin' to hate the little bastard.

Thought That Just Popped Into My Head:
Whose uglier? Yasser Arafat or
Camilla Parker Bowles?

Cheney invited me to lunch. Thought he was gonna fire me, but right after the first course I realized he worked for me & that he couldn't fire me. He kept makin' this creepy small talk. From readin' The <u>Art of War</u> I knew he was up to somethin'. Finally, after my third bowl of Chunky Monkey he laid it on me. Wanted to know if I'd mind if he & I shared the Oval Office. Couldn't believe it. I jumped at the chance. Now I won't never be alone no more.

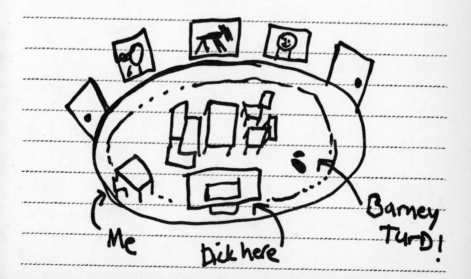

Me   Dick here   Barney TurD!

Monday, March 12, 2001

This is the steady hand that controls the nucular button of the United States of America. And I know it's a steady hand because it's, I mean, was, my beer-holdin' hand. Never spilled a drop!

Note To Self: Seein' as I'm President & the most powerful man in the world, do I have to ask myself for permission to take a day off now & then?

A leader has to know how to act in any situation & I was tested again today. A Boy Scout Troop was takin' a tour of the White House & one a them little peckerheads started hecklin' me, sayin' I stole the election & that Gore should be President. But I didn't lose my kewl. I stayed very calm & gave him the Official Presidential Middle Finger Salute.

Note To Self: Find out what RNC stands for.

It's gettin' harder & harder to keep our kids outa the spotlight. Last night Jenna told me she met a boy at the White House gate. 'Course I had him captured & taken to Quantico for interrogation. Turns out he was a reporter for the _National Enquirer_. We finally let him go, but not 'til he spilled the beans about which movie stars have had hooter implants.

Laura's been makin' me read Shakespeare. All them weird rhymes & that Elizabeth Taylor pentameter crap's drivin' me nuts. Found one sentence, though, that got me thinkin': "Uneasy lies the head that wears the crown." Wonder what that means.

Holy shit! I forgot to file my income tax return.

False alarm on the tax thing. Got another month.

(Note To Self) Start a list of people who should be audited by the IRS.

Al Gore

David Boies

Florida Supreme Court

Jeb

Christine Todd Whitman (if Barney don't get housebroken by the end a the month)

College kids'll be goin' on their Spring Breaks soon. Wish Commanders in Chief got Spring Breaks.
  I remember Fort Lauderdale back in the '60s. Wet T-shirt contests, Kegger parties, horny co-eds comin' on to me after they found out I came from oil money.

Been thinkin' about creatin' a new National Holiday so I, I mean, the poor workin' stiffs, can get another day off. We got all them Jewish holidays, Labor Day for the workin' stiffs, Martin Luther King for black people to take off. Why not somethin' for people like me? White guys who rose to positions of power because of family connections. We could close all the schools & businesses for a day, but keep all the bars & golf courses open 'round the clock.

St. Patrick's Day. Even though my ancestors come from England and we hate the Irish, this used to be my favorite day a the year. Sure would like some green beer & a little Jameson. One sip wouldn't hurt. But how? Who can I call? Nobody on my staff. Nobody in my family. Only one hope. D.Q.

Sunday, March 18, 2001

Got back from Betty Ford in one piece. Ran into all kinds of movie stars there. Most of 'em were liberal Democrats. None of 'em knew it was me. Poppy called Chuck Heston & arranged for some Hollywood make-up guy to disguise me. Told everybody I was Ozzy Osbourne.

Been the Leader of the Free World now for 60 days. I don't feel like a President. Feel more like a sidekick on a talk show.

Note To Self: Call Ed McMahon, Andy Richter & that bald guy on Larry Sanders.

Wednesday, March 21, 2001

~~I'm sure this journal will fall into the hands of future historians so I want to make one point very clearly. I couldn't do this job without Dick Cheney. In fact, I often wonder why I'm the president and he isn't. The country would be in much better hands with him in control.~~

Damn! I knew Cheney'd been secretly readin' my diary! Now I gotta find another hiding place!

I'm getting' really tired a hearin' "Hail To the Chief" every time I walk into some fancy sitdown at the White House. I think it's time we got a new anthem around here. So far I came up with 4 possibilities:

• "Help"

• The theme song to <u>Scarface</u>: where Al Pacino snorted tons of cocaine then did some really crazy things in Florida

• "Take This Job & Shove It"

• "The *Name Game*" (Bush, Bush Bo-Bush, Bananafana fo fush fee fi fo fush... Bush. GO BUSH!)

I think Strom Thurmond's gettin' senile. He was wearin' a T-shirt that said "Viagra For President."

Feelin' good today. Have a real sense of accomplishment. Finally got somethin' done. Trained Barney to crap on the paper.

It was finally payback time for New York City. They voted big-time for Gore. So yesterday Cheney & I did an official flyover on Air Force One. Hey, New York, that full moon in the sky was mine!

Need to slow down today. Stayed up late messin' around with the new PlayStation 2 that my main Secret Service guy gave me. He let me hold his gun. Wonder if there's a greetin' card 'specially for Secret Service agents. Like, "I hope you're feeling better after gettin' shot & losin' all mobility in your body. Stay in touch!"

Not much to do today so at D.Q.'s suggestion, I been makin' lists. He said that's how he killed time when he was Poppy's VP. I call this one <u>Why You Should Be Concerned That I'm President.</u>

- I can start a thermonucular World War.

- I can give away billions of dollars of taxpayer's money to the rich.

- I'm the most powerful person in the world & you aren't.

- I'm feelin' absolutely no guilt about any a this & you're startin' to get a queasy twitch in the pit of your stomach that's gonna get worse & worse for the next coupla years 'til you suddenly wake up in the middle a the night & come to the catastrophic realization that votin' for me was the single worse decision you ever made in your unfortunate, misguided, white-trash life.

- Have a nice day!

Saw "Senator" Hillary comin' outa her new townhouse with her unemployed hubby. Keep thinkin' about the $8 mil she got for her memoirs. Wonder how much I'll get for mine.

Note To Self: Find out what you're supposed to put in a memoir.

Further Note To Self: Wait a minute. I thought a memoir was one a them big clunky pieces a furniture you hang your clothes in or hide your stash in. Check the dictionary.

Thing To Do: Get a dictionary.

Jeb & I are on good terms again. Bein' a Christian I forgave him for nearly blowin' it in Florida. Invited him to this hoity-toity party we're throwin' at the White House as a way a hustlin', I mean, reachin' out to young African-American multimillioniares.

Had another meetin' with my Drug Czar. I look forward to 'em because whenever he asks me anything I always have the right answer.

Had my first meetin' with my space advisers. Boy was I embarrassed. They were here to talk about funding for a new interplanetary defense program. I thought we were gonna talk about makin' more room at the Texas White House.

Problems to the left! Problems to the right! Stand up! Sit down! Fight! Fight! FIGHT! Whenever I get down, a good old-fashioned cheer gets me goin' again. 'Specially if I do it with pom-poms.

Hey, I liked bein' a cheerleader at Yale. Everybody did what you told 'em to do & you never got hurt. Kinda like bein' a President.

Wednesday, March 28, 2001

Had to meet with the new Senators which meant that "Senator" Hillary was here. Made eye contact with her for about a second. I swear, haven't been that scared by a woman since I sat next to Arianna Huffington in Larry King's Green Room.

If Barney takes a whiz on my journal one more time I'm gonna drown him in the Potomac.

Get more No-Doz!

* Note To Self: Find out if No-Doz can be ordered by the gross.

...ugh: Fatboy... ... use portrait to use for target practice.

Thing To Do: Invite Sean "Puffy" Combs to the young African-American multi-millionaire bash. Tell him to bring Jennifer Lopez so Jeb's wife'll have somebody to talk to.

Just dawned on me. It's the same year as Stanley Kubricks's neat movie <u>2001:</u> <u>A Space Odyssey</u>. Saw it back in 1968 with the cheerleadin' squad. We all were scared & stoned & musta spent three days discussin' what that damn monolith symbolized. I didn't say much. Heck, I was tryin' to figure out what the word monolith meant.

Thing To Do: Find out just what the hell "monolith" does mean.

Potomac.

Saturday, March 31, 2001

The only thing I like about Cokey Roberts is her first name.

People been talkin' about that Tecumseh's Revenge thing. That's the theory that any President elected in a year endin' with a O won't finish his term. Shit. Hope that happens to me.

Had lunch with my buds in the NRA. Wish we coulda met at my ranch in Crawford, I mean, the Texas White House. Shit, I love sayin' that. We coulda gone huntin'. Gave them good ole boys a Kewl gift though: Fatboy's official White House portrait to use for target practice.

THE WHITE HOUSE
WASHINGTON, D. C.

TO DO

1. Read a book without pictures.

2. Be nicer to poor people & all have-nots in general.

3. Think before I speak & only use words I know how to pronounce.

4. Stop suckin' my teeth during Cabinet meetings.

5. Stop fallin' down in front of the Secret Service & screamin' "I've been hit!"

6. Start takin' this whole President thing more seriously.

APRIL FOOLS DAY!
Gotcha, you freakin' historians.

Monday, April 2, 2001

Since my ancestors come from British royalty, I been readin' up on them old Kings & Princes & Dukes of Earl. Pretty dangerous times. They all had a guy whose job it was to eat some of their food to make sure nobody was tryin' to poison 'em. Wonder if I need one a them guys.

Thing To Do: Find out if Gore's still lookin' for work. Maybe he'll do it.

Met with Strom Thurmond today. He's an <u>old</u> fucker!

YADA

Thing To Do: Find out what the hell yada means.

Note To Historians: Nobody in the world knows what yada means.

* Possible legacy for me. Be the person who figured out what yada means.

Laura & I spent the weekend at Camp David. It was an OK place 'cept for the name. Sounds like one of those Kibbutz things Jews go to in Israel. Kennebunkport. Now that's a name. And it's easy to remember cuz when I was a kid my friend Kenny & I used to get drunk all the time & pass out on the bunks in my room.

Found out that Eisenhower named Camp David after his grandson, David. Wouldn't it have been a hoot if he had a granddaughter & he named it after her & her name was Condoleezza?

I like to keep things simple & right now this is how I feel. Big-time happy. Because I finally stopped giggling about this whole President thing when I'm alone. From now on I just wanna smile about it & take it one day at a time like I learned in the 12-Step Program.

Friday, April 6, 2001

Three months from today's my 55th birthday. Wouldn't it be Kewl if everybody in America sent me a birthday card? Then I could make a big bonfire outa them & blow it out like one big candle. Maybe C-SPAN would cover it.

So glad Laura doesn't want to be co-President like "Senator" Hillary. Laura's a great wife & a great librarian. She's also a great mom to me. Oh yeah & to our daughters, Barbara & Jenna.

Met with Strom Thurmond again. Pushy SOB. He looks like Yoda from Star Wars.

Thing To Pursue: Wonder if Yada comes from Yoda?

War is hell. That's why I don't wanna start
one. I remember seein' this mushroom thing
in a movie when I was a kid. The government
exploded a nucular bomb & it turned
all the ants in the desert into giant monsters.

Why I don't wanna start a war!

Jerry Falwell stopped by today. He looks like a fat Phil Donahue. He told me that God likes me better than Gore. I like Jerry.

Found out that _Mad_ magazine's gonna put my face on the cover of their next issue & that got me steamed. Everybody's always makin fun a me! But I'm a leader so we worked out a deal.

Monday, April 9, 2001

Lotsa important stuff happened today, but I can't talk about it. That's cuz I was hypnotized by the CIA & I'm startin' to hear a little voice in my head. The voice wants me to call it Master.

That <u>West Wing</u> TV show is such a turd. Not real at all. Martin Sheen acts like he's in control. People don't tell him what to do or say. I ain't watchin' it no more. I like my TV grounded in reality & true to life like 3rd <u>Rock From the Sun</u>.

Note To Self: If the Poppy movie can't be a feature & we can't get big stars, maybe it could be one a them Movies of the Week & Martin Sheen could play Poppy, Charley Sheen could play me & Tom Arnold could play Jeb.

Note To Self: Find out how Charley Sheen & Emelio Estevez can be brothers but have different last names.

Mother called to lecture me about my
posture, my haircut & the way I squint
when I get confused. Poppy said to ignore her.
"You're President of the United States. You
don't have to listen to your mother or me or
anybody anymore. Except Cheney."

Note To Historians: I'm proud as all hell that
I achieved some Presidential "firsts" already.
My advisers tell me I'm the first President
ever to wear a clip-on tie to a State Dinner,
give the original cast of Hee-Haw the
Presidential Medal of Honor & ask the Prime
Minister of France "How's it hangin'?"

Hi. It's Laura. I've seen you writing in this journal and I was wondering what it was. I don't have time now, but I want to go through it and correct your misspellings, punctuation, and grammar. By the way, I don't think I look like a librarian at all! I always thought I looked like a stern teacher who's going to be waiting for her naughty little Georgie tonight so she can teach him a lesson. That's right. Mommy is mad. And when Mommy gets mad George has to do some naughty things.

P.S. Wear those cute little boxer shorts with the armadillos on them.

Friday the 13th. Never realized how scary the White House could be until today. I was mindin' my own business, strollin' through the East Wing, lookin' for Spot cuz Barney was tryin' to hump him & he ran away. I bumped into what I was sure was a horrifyin' ghost. Then I realized it was Strom Thurmond.

Cheney says I need to go to Israel. Hope they don't make me wear one a them yarmulkes. And if I gotta eat any a that matza stuff I know I'll barf.

Personal Observation: Is it my imagination or does Jesse Ventura look he could be the child of Telly Savalas & Janet Reno?

Note To Historians: Here's a little background info on how decisions really get made at the White House:

- Flip a coin
- Ouijii board
- Call Poppy
- Close the door to the Oval Office & ask myself what the greatest leader of the 20th century would do in the same situation: James T. Kirk, Captain of the Starship Enterprise

Thing To Do: Ask Rush Limbaugh if he lost all that flab cuz he had an eating problem, like I used to have a problem with blow. Ask Rush if his wife had to hide the Twinkies like Laura hid my stash.

Easter Sunday. We're havin' an Easter egg
hunt in the Rose Garden for poor kids.
Karl Rove said I could hide the eggs & that later
I could dress up like the Easter Bunny. I
just hope the real Easter Bunny doesn't get mad.

Wonder why they name all the rooms in the
White House after Presidents anyway?
I never even heard a half them guys.

Cheney & Rove put the kabash on another one
a my ideas for what I should be remembered
for. What's wrong with wantin' to be the
guy responsible for legalizin' cocaine?

Monday, April 16, 2001

Met with the Joint Chiefs of Staff today.
Asked them if this whole gays-in-the-military
thing was workin' out. I didn't understand
their answer. Then I asked them if they
had any naked pictures of guys wrestlin' each
other during basic training. They said they'd
get back to me.

Found out that if I use the Hot Line
to make regular calls they can't be traced.
Sometimes when I'm bored I'll call Presidents,
Kings, Prime Ministers & leaders of other
countries & just say

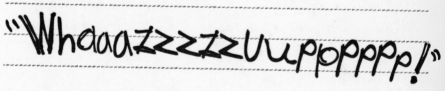

"Whaazzzzzuuppppp!"

Wednesday, April 18, 2001

Note To Historians: Didn't write anything in the journal yesterday. Don't be alarmed. I was on the job as usual being a leader. But the White House is a very big place. I got confused. And a leader can lose things just like anybody else.

Big press conference tomorrow. Cheney & Rove told me to bone up on economics facts, 'specially the difference between a recession & a depression. Hell, that's easy. A recession is bad times & a depression is really bad times.

Note To Self: Wonder where the expression "bone up" came from.

Big problems on the homefront. May have to write Dear Abby a note. Anyhoo, Laura & Mother haven't been gettin' along since we moved to Washington, primarily because she & "Senator" Hillary are becomin' friends. Mother keeps remindin' Laura that Hillary's out-of-work husband beat Poppy & that the Clintons will always be our ENEMY. Laura says it's unhealthy to hold grudges. I told her that holdin' grudges is what bein' a Bush is all about.

Internal Reflection: Damn, I hate it when Laura makes me wonder about things.

Friday, April 20, 2001

Last night was really awesome. All my old
frat brothers from Delta Kappa Epsilon
came by to celebrate my 90th day as
President. I couldn't chug beers with 'em
anymore, but I still puked in the toilet
for old time's sake. Then we went up on
the roof & "watered" the rose bushes.

Dreamed about Tom DeLay last night. Only
instead of bein' the little pipsqueak he normally
is he was 7 feet tall. He barged into the
Oval Office lookin' like a Chucky doll on steroids
rantin' & ravin' about kickin' my Presidential
ass unless I start signin' his stupid bills.
Lucky for me that Condoleezza was there or
I woulda been toast. While I was hidin' under
my desk, she decked him.

Saturday, April 21, 2001

Major bummer. Nobody wants to make a movie about Poppy. Nobody! And not one star is interested in playin' him or me, although Tom Arnold has said yes to Jeb.

Maybe consider producin' Poppy's movie myself. Make one a them independent films. Maybe call those two Jews who run Maxamira. Only problem is, they're Liberals. Probably won't take my call. What the heck, I'm the President. They'll take my call.

Note To Self: Put Bob & Harvey Weinstein, every Maxamira employee & every person who ever worked on a Maxamira movie on my To-Be-Audited list.

Sunday, April 22, 2001

Today's Earth Day. Gore & all them tree huggers are out there protestin' that I'm screwin' up the environment. But I'm not. I love the environment because that's where you find all the wild animals that I love to hunt & kill.

Bob Dole keeps buggin' me about findin' his wife Liddy a job in my Administration. What the hell do they need money for? Dole's got family bucks from that pineapple company.

Thing To Ponder: Dole's wife's first name is the same as G. Gordon Liddy's last name. If she married him her name would be Liddy Liddy.

Monday, April 23, 2001

Got some hate mail from MENSA.
They're the club you gotta be really brainy to join.
They said my public speakin' is an embarrassment
to the country. Screw them!

THE WHITE HOUSE
WASHINGTON, D. C.

Dear Pointy-Headed A-holes:

Book-learnin' is overrated. So let's settle
this once & for all. Stop writin' me. All
them big words give me headaches &
hurt my eyes & make me squint even
more. I may not be smart enough to
qualify for MENSA, but I got some
better initials at my disposal: FBI, CIA
& IRS for starters.

Best wishes,

W.

Tuesday, April 24, 2001

Cheney & Rove brought in this hotshot voice Coach from Yale Drama School. They say I sound like the President of a 4-H Club, not President of a Superpower. Jeez, I feel like Eliza Doolittle in that movie _Pretty Woman._ "The rain . . . in Spain . . . my ass." Gotta go now. My tongue needs a nap!

The Christian Right is startin' to get on my nerves. Pat Robertson keeps callin' me with all these crazy ideas. He wants to bring back chastity belts, town hangings & burning people at the stake.

Thing To Do: Call Robertson after lunch, my nap & _Guiding Light_ & tell him to chill! He's startin' to make organized religion look like WWF wrestling.

Grace, my psychic adviser, is startin' to creep me out. She says that someone in my inner circle is untrustworthy. She couldn't come up with a name, but she says it rhymes with "rainy." So far I can't figure out who it could be.

I remember when Elvis showed up at the White House gates to visit Nixon. They spent like 2 hours together just shootin' the shit, then Nixon appointed him an official agent for the DAE, I mean, DEA. Heck, if Elvis showed up to see me we'da gotten so wasted it'd be like a Grateful Dead concert.

Thursday, April 26, 2001

Performed the Heimlich maneuver on Cheney yesterday. My cat India thought he was snarlin' at her so she attacked him. Somehow one a her fur balls got lodged in his throat. When I was applyin' pressure to his solar plexus I had my arms around him.

Private Thought: Felt like I was huggin' the Michelin Man.

Note To Historians: I don't think Cheney wears underwear.

I heard that voice in my head again last night when I was sayin' my prayers. It sounded whiny & creepy like Joe Lieberman. It said something about me being a pawn, but I don't play chess. Yahtsi is my game. Maybe the CIA's gonna teach me how to play chess.

Finally accomplished somethin' big! I knew I could be a movie producer. Managed to find 3 people interested in playin' Poppy, me & Jeb in Poppy's movie (providin' they get script approval).

Poppy: Rudy from Survivor
Me: Danny Bonaduce

Jeb: Carrot Top (if Tom Arnold can't do it)

Saturday, April 28, 2001

Tomorrow marks the end of my first 100 days on the job. Feels like I been here a million days. The voice in my head is gettin' louder. It's makin' me do things. I'm tryin' to fight back, but I can't. I'm too weak. I'm just little Georgie Bush from Crawford, Texas. Why did I want to become President? This is all a terrible mistake. Maybe it's a dream. I'll pinch myself. Ouch! Damn! Ain't no dream. OK.

I gotta stop. The voice is tellin' me to shut up & start a war. I have to go now.

365 (days in a year)

×4

1460

−100 (time already served)

1360

−56 (2 weeks vacation per year)

1304

−40 (sick days, 10 per year)

1264

−4 (birthdays)

1260 (days to go)

No way I can handle this! Gore can have it. Cheney can have it. I'm not the President. I demand a recount! Call Lily. Call Scalia. Call Jeb. I demand a recount! I demand a recount!!!

THE END

The PReZ
George W. Bush

THE PRESIDENT

George W.

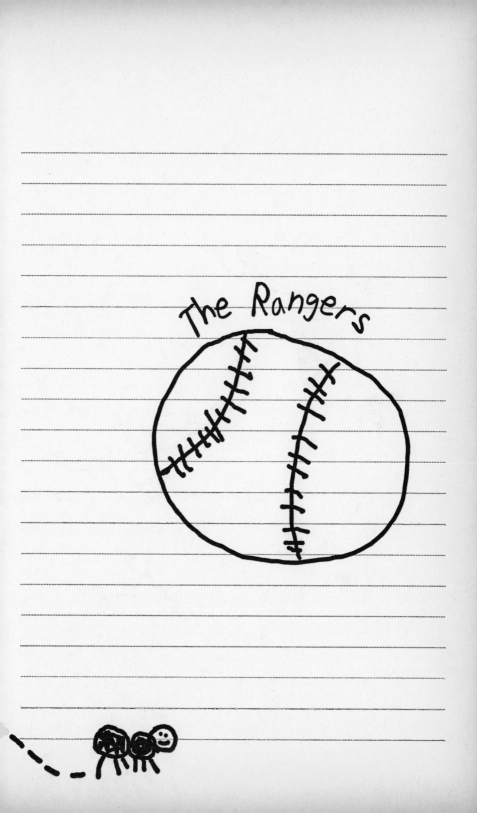

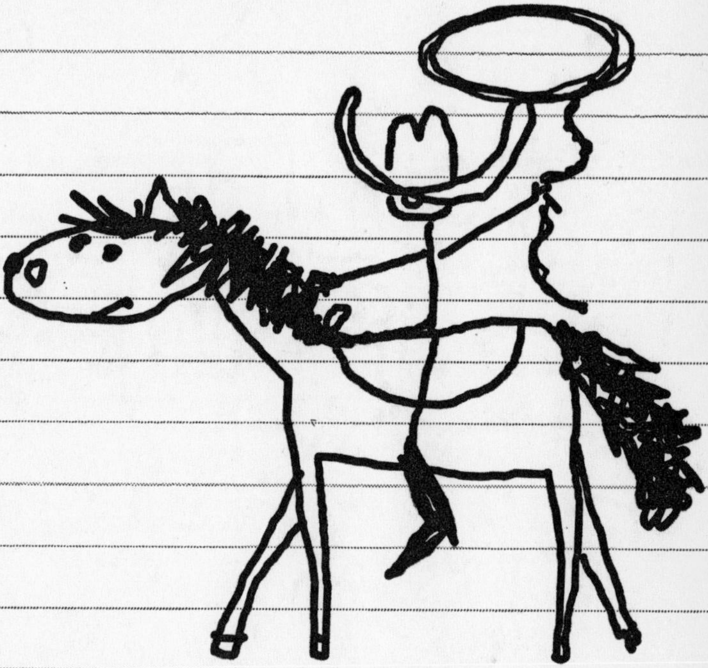

About the Authors

D. B. Gilles is the author of *The Screenwriter Within: How to Turn the Movie in Your Head into a Salable Screenplay*. He teaches screenwriting and comedy writing at New York University's Tisch School of the Arts in the Department of Dramatic Writing and the Film & Television Department. He has written for the screen, stage, and TV, and his work has been published in the *New York Times*.

Sheldon Woodbury teaches screenwriting, playwriting, and video in New York University's Tisch School of the Arts in the Department of Dramatic Writing. He has sold short stories, worked in children's television, written award-winning screenplays, and has had several of his plays produced in New York City.

Contact the authors at Wfirst100days@aol.com.